Ray Reardon's 50 BEST TRICK SHOTS

BEST TRICK
SHOTS

DAVID & CHARLES
Newton Abbot   London   North Pomfret (Vt)

ISBN 07153 7993 3

Reardon, Ray
  Ray Reardon's 50 best trick shots.
  1. Snooker
  I. Ainsworth, Brian   II. 50 best trick shots
  III. Fifty best trick shots
  794.7'3   GV900.S6

Printed in Great Britain
by A Wheaton & Co Ltd, Hennock Way, Exeter
for David & Charles (Publishers) Limited
Brunel House Newton Abbot Devon

Published in the United States of America
by David & Charles Inc
North Pomfret Vermont 05053 USA

Contents

Introduction

When I was asked to write the introduction for this book, I was naturally delighted, as the Alliss family have been devotees of the game of snooker for more years than any of us would care to remember, and my father Percy was a particular friend of the great Joe Davis. Snooker is one of those games which blossomed in popularity, almost overnight; suddenly everyone wanted to watch and play. I became more involved in the game since my early meeting with Ray which, strangely enough, took place on the golf course at Gleneagles, during the Pro-Celebrity Golf Series for the *BBC*. I think he would be the first to admit that his snooker is just a touch better than his golf!

His skills have already delighted me and millions of other people, and I am sure that this book of fascinating trick shots will give hours of pleasure to many more of us.

Peter Alliss
July 1980

Party Tricks

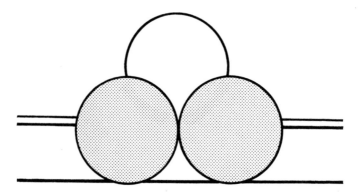

1 Missed it . . . No I haven't   This trick is easy to do and a lot of fun.

Place the two red balls against the cushion and then balance the yellow on top, so that it is supported by both the reds and the cushion. Then place the cue ball at the other end of the table. Next explain that you are going to play the cue ball on to the yellow without hitting the reds — which, of course, seems to be impossible.

Simply strike the cue ball with only enough power to just reach the yellow. When it has travelled half the length of the table, exclaim 'Missed it'; bang your fist on the table, and the vibration will cause the yellow to drop on to the table just before the cue ball arrives.

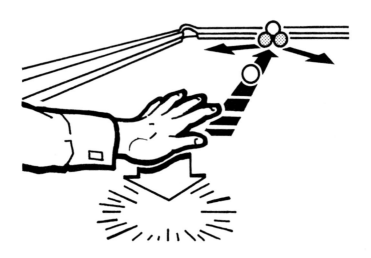

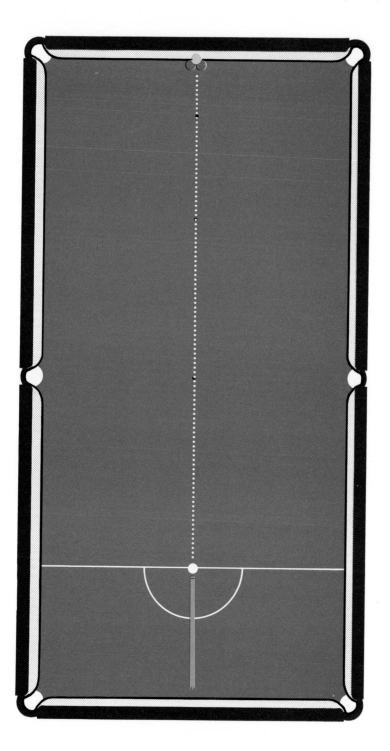

2 Train shot   A trick that entertains the children.

Position the cues on the table so that the tip of the cue furthest from the cushion is opposite the centre pocket, then position the other cue parallel but with the tip slightly further back — see the illustration.

Explain that the cue ball is the engine and the red balls the coaches, and place them on top of the cues. All the balls will roll gently into the pocket one by one.

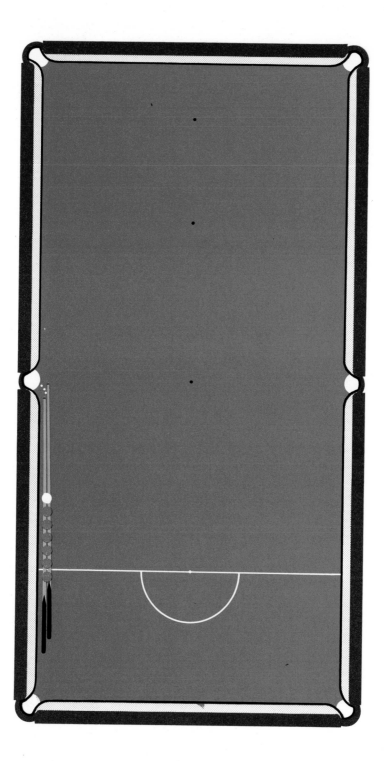

3 Snake shot Another easy trick to do.

First position the black and the nearest red to it so that they are in line with the pocket. Then place all the other reds, in any shape you like, so that they are not more than half a ball's width apart from each other.

The principle of the shot is obvious from the illustration; the cue ball strikes one red on to the next, and so on, until the last red knocks the black into the pocket. The shot needs to be played with plenty of power.

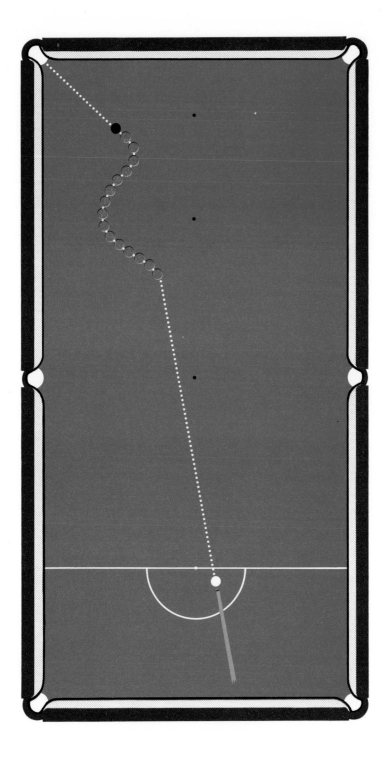

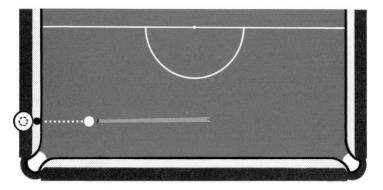

4 Coin into the glass This shot is easy on some tables and difficult on others — it depends on the flexibility of the cushion.

Place a glass on the edge of the table and a coin next to it on the cushion. Strike the ball fairly hard at the cushion and the coin will jump up into the air and land in the glass.

5 Match trick At first glance this shot looks easy, but see if you can do it.

Three reds are placed so that they touch each other and a match stick is then positioned vertically in the centre. You will find it easier to get the match stick to stand up if you damp the end.

Place the cue ball anywhere you like and try to knock the match down. You will find that however strongly you play the shot, the match will only fall down if the shot is played as a run-though — in other words, the cue ball must follow through to knock the match over.

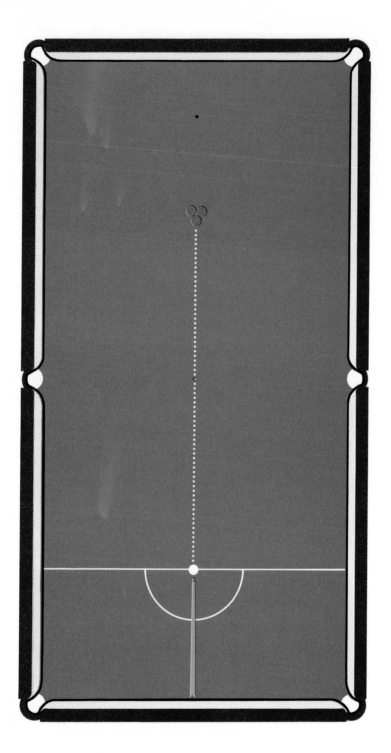

6 Surprise pocket   You will need to have a jacket on, and somebody standing by to catch the ball in case you miss.

Place two balls right on the lip of the corner pockets and the cue ball in the centre of the 'D'. Now challenge your opponent to pocket all three balls in one shot.

The trick is done by putting two cues on the table (see the illustration) so that the butt ends are touching the two balls. Play the cue ball straight up the table so that it comes off the top cushion, back down the table and hits the cues. The impact will cause the two balls to be pocketed, while the cue ball will jump off the table — you nimbly catch it in your jacket pocket.

R.R.T.S.—B

7 Three-ball challenge   Get your opponent to stand next to a centre pocket, then place a red ball on the edge of the pocket and the pink and brown balls on their spots.

Now challenge the person to pot all three balls without moving their feet.

To demonstrate how this shot can be done, stand in the same place, reverse the cue so that you can pot the red by playing towards yourself. Then, holding the end of the cue firmly on the table, swing the butt end to left and right so that it hits the pink and brown into the pockets.

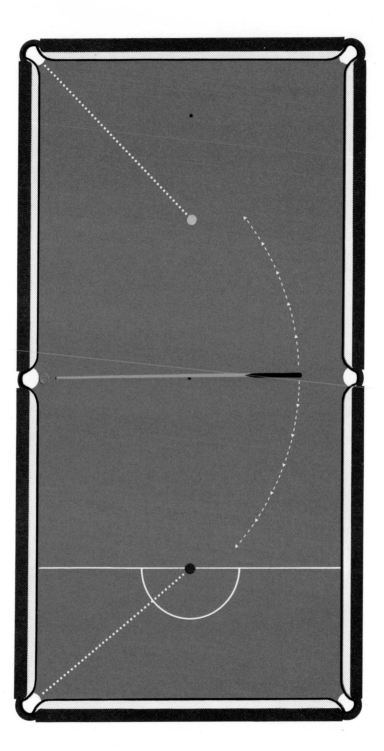

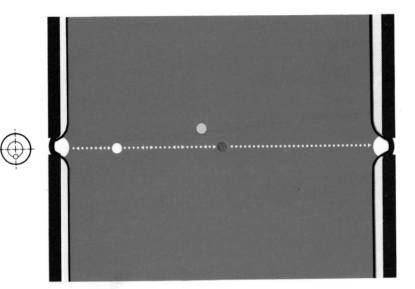

8 Kiss shot You are going to pot the red into the centre pocket, screw back the cue ball into the opposite pocket, and kiss the yellow into its own pocket. With the balls positioned as they are in the illustration this would be quite impossible. Strike the cue ball low down to impart plenty of back spin and pot the red. The cue ball will then screw back into the opposite centre pocket. Pick up the yellow ball, touch it to your lips and drop it into its own pocket!

9 Coin shot This stunt looks easier than it really is. Place a ball over one of the corner pockets and try to knock it in using a 10p piece instead of the cue ball. With practice you will be able to judge the right amount of strength to play the shot.

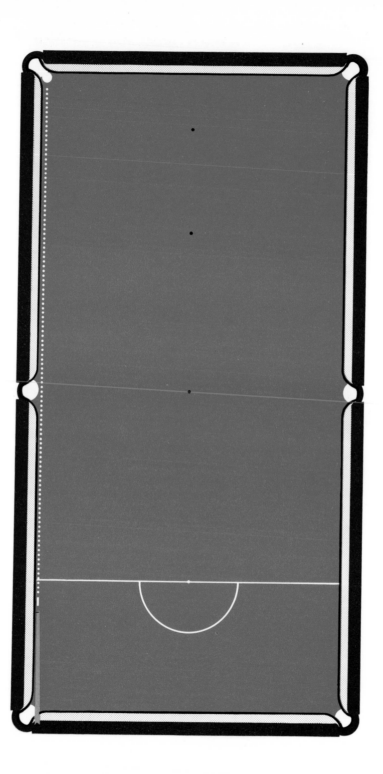

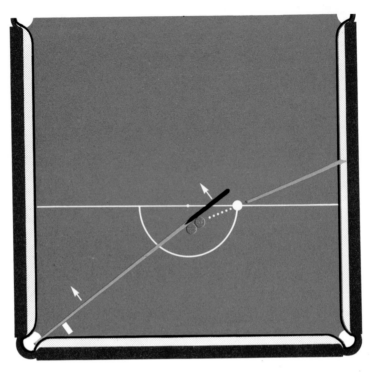

10 Match-box trick Put a cue on the table — as indicated in the illustration — with the tip against the corner pocket cushion. Then place the two reds in position (touching each other and the cue); finally, snooker yourself with a match-box or a packet of cigarettes.

The object is to pot the red nearest the pocket without knocking over the match-box.

The shot needs to be played with some strength, striking the cue ball towards the nearer red. This red will move the cue out of the way and set the other red on its way to the pocket — and it goes down without knocking the match-box over.

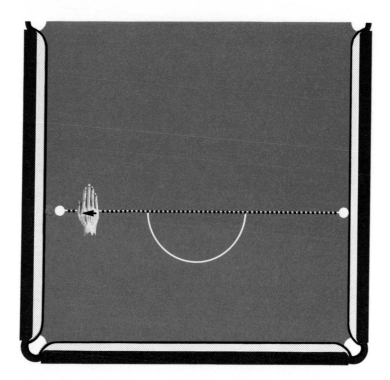

11 A handy trick   Place a red ball against the cushion on the
baulk line, with the cue ball touching it as shown in the illustration. The third ball is placed at the other end of the baulk
line.
Hit the *red* ball a glancing blow with the palm of your hand.
This makes the cue ball double back along the baulk line to
cannon on to the other white.

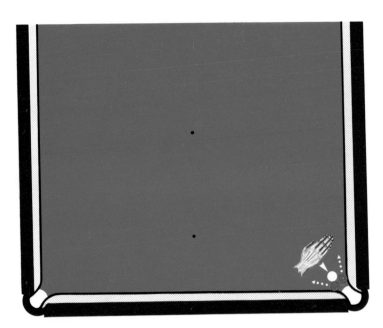

12 In-off by hand The principle of this trick is similar to the previous one.

The two reds are placed tight together in a corner pocket, and the white then jammed against the two reds. This time strike the white ball with the palm of your hand, which will cause all three balls to rebound away from the pocket, but the spin imparted to the white ball will make it double back into the pocket.

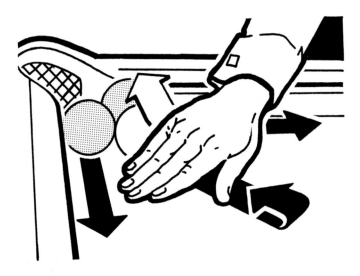

Snooker Trick Shots

13 Impossible yellow   The object is to pot the yellow into the top right-hand pocket, despite being apparently snookered. If you look carefully at the illustration you will see that the shot is not as difficult as it looks. The cue ball is screwed off the loose red to strike the other red which has been planted against the yellow. The loose red then hits the first ball in the semi-circle, which, providing all the reds in the semi-circle are touching each other, causes the last red to move out of the way so that the yellow can get to the pocket.

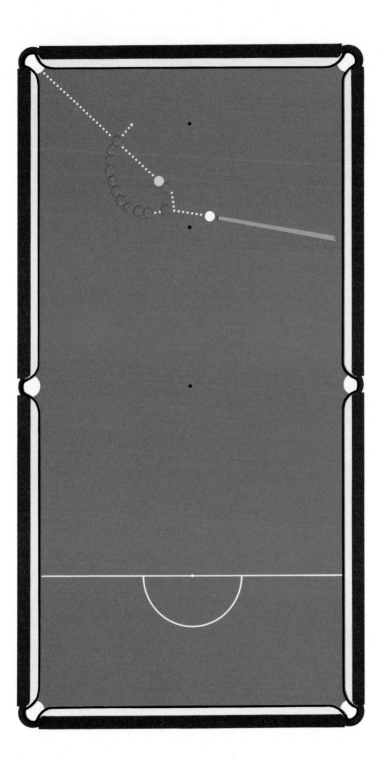

14 Rat-tat-tat   The row of reds should be spaced a fraction more than a ball's width away from the cushion. Aim to hit the cue ball — using strong right-hand side — on to the cushion rather than off the leading red.

The cue ball will zig-zag between the cushion and the reds all the way to the black, which is then potted.

This shot is easier than it looks and the positioning of the cue ball is not that critical.

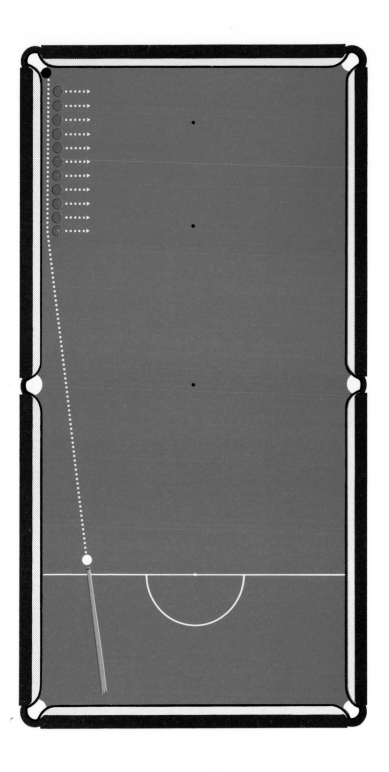

15 Three ways to pot black In the position shown in the illustration there are three possible methods of potting the black:

1 Strike the cue ball, using right-hand side, at the angle of the pocket. This will bring the cue ball back along the top cushion to pot the black.

2 Play the cue ball down the table to come off the bottom cushion.

3 Try going all round the cushions.

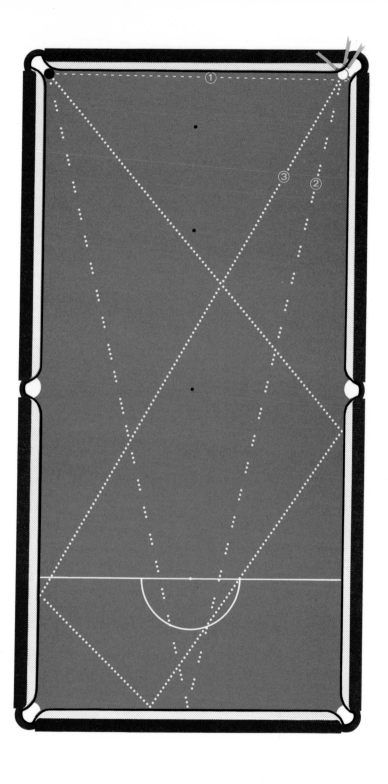

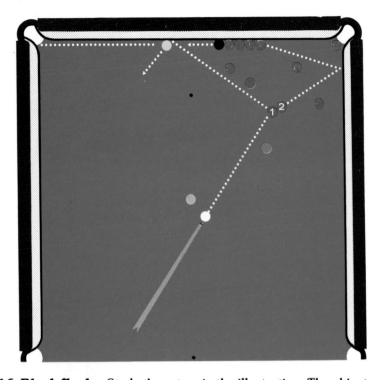

16 Black flash   Study the set-up in the illustration. The object
is to pot the black in the right-hand corner pocket.
The row of reds and the black are all touching each other
and against the cushion. The yellow is one inch away from
the cushion so that it is between the black and the pocket.
Position Nos 1 and 2 reds so that No 2 red will come off the
cushion into the row of reds and so get the black moving
towards the pocket. The cue ball is screwed off No 1 red on to
the yellow, taking it away from the cushion. Other balls in
the illustration are just there to make the shot look more difficult than it really is.

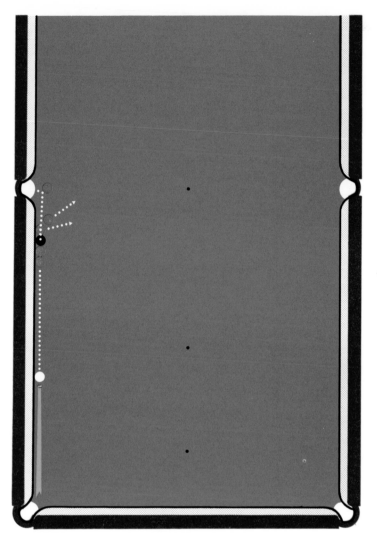

17 Black into centre pocket Position the balls as indicated in the illustration. The three reds and the black must be touching each other and right against the cushion.
Strike the cue ball low down and straight at the nearest red — unless the red is struck in the centre the trick will not work. The leading red in the row will hit the loose red next to it, causing both of them to make way for the black to go in-off the red over the centre pocket.

18 Demon red   Not an easy shot to make this one. It needs to be played with power.

The loose red is played hard into the pack so that it is deflected down the table and into the bottom right-hand pocket.

Note that three of the reds in the pack are aligned with a point just short of the pocket (see arrow) and that along the points of impact the reds are arranged in a semi-circle.

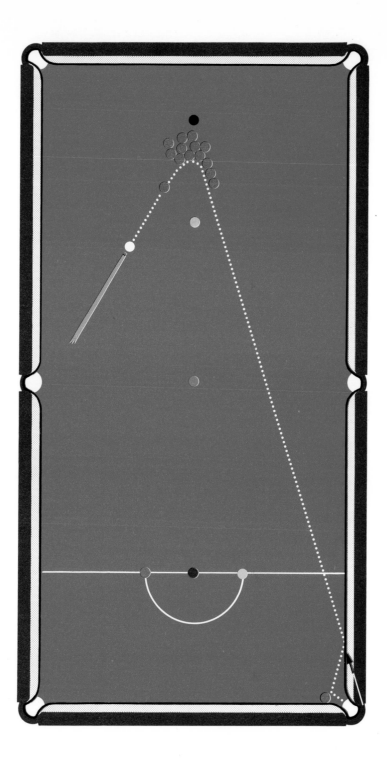

19 Blue surprise The object is to pot the blue into the left centre pocket.

Position the balls as set up in the illustration — note that the five reds furthest from the baulk line are all in a straight line. Strike the cue ball with plenty of top spin making thick contact with the red, and lots of follow-through to take the blue along. The second red — the one further from the cue ball — will proceed towards the pocket ahead of the blue, clearing the three pairs of reds out of the way for the blue to go into the pocket.

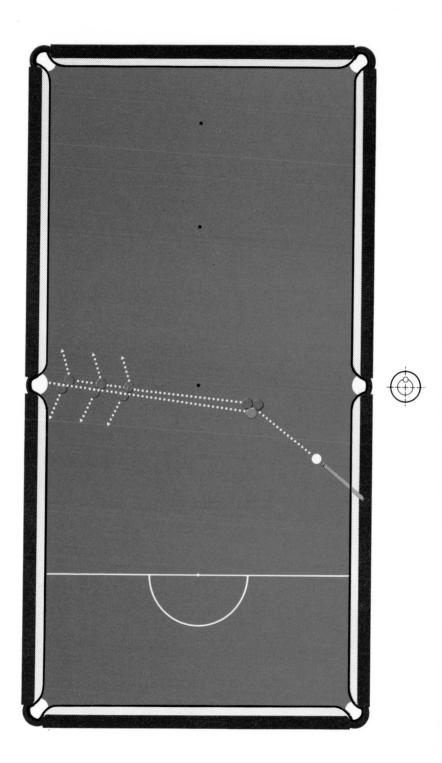

20 Deflecting shot   Here you are going to pot all four colours with one shot. It is not as difficult as it looks, and certainly easier than the last two trick shots.

In setting up the shot, make sure that the yellow and the three reds next to it are all touching and aligned with the opposite centre pocket.

Strike the cue ball below centre, using plenty of power, to make contact with Nos 1 and 2 reds evenly. The yellow goes into the centre pocket; No 1 red goes up the table to pot the green; No 3 red goes across the table to pot the brown; No 2 red comes off the top cushion, back down the table and is deflected off the row of reds towards the blue.

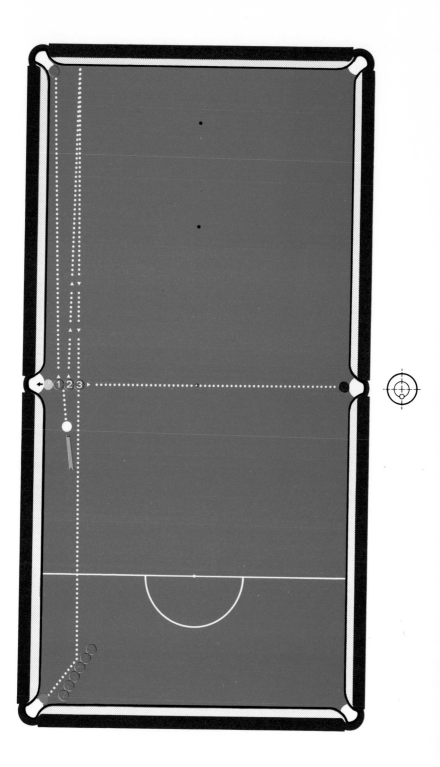

21 Four colour shot Using deep screw and left-hand side, the cue ball must strike the red left of centre to screw back to the brown. However, if you haven't mastered this technique, you can try a straightforward shot using only the three other colours.

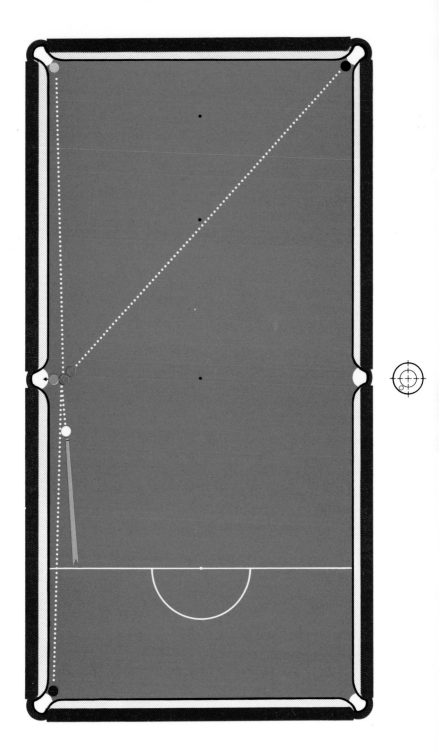

22 Three reds trick Having placed two reds over opposite corner pockets, position the third red slightly away from the cushion with the black touching it.

Use strong left-hand side so that the cue ball comes off the black and then off three cushions to pot the red over the yellow pocket. The black pots the red over the top pocket and the third red is doubled across the table into the opposite centre pocket.

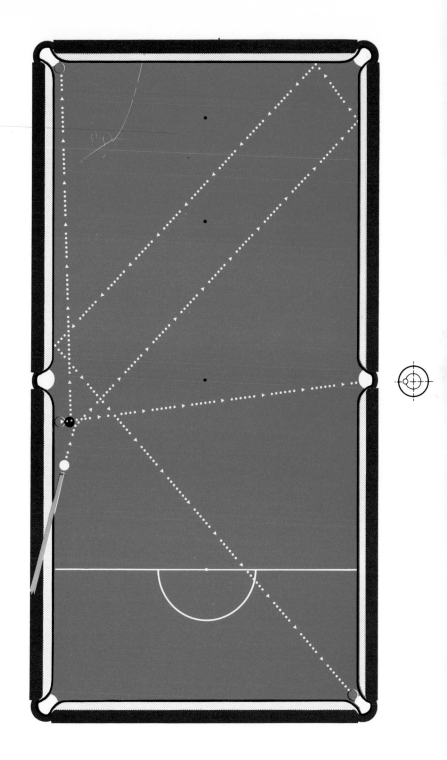

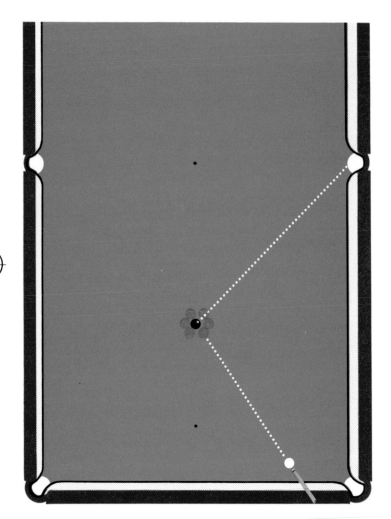

23 Super black One of my favourite shots this, but not an easy one.

The object is to pot the black into the centre pocket.

Place the black on the pink spot and then arrange the reds around it in two groups of three; each group of reds must be touching each other. Using deep screw, strike the cue ball hard at the nearest red to hit it left of centre. The black will then be deflected off the furthest red towards the centre pocket.

You will see that the black is deflected almost at a right angle from the direction the cue ball is played. It is therefore possible by repositioning the cue ball to pot the black into any of the four top pockets.

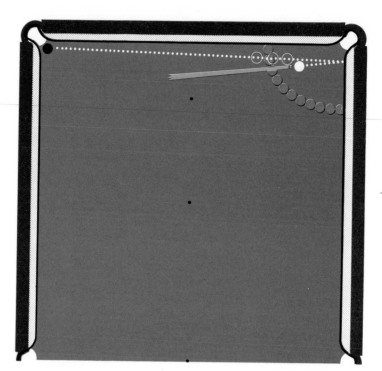

24 On the rebound In this position the black can only be potted by getting the cue ball to jump over the circle of reds. Strike the cue ball slightly below centre and towards the cushion. The cue ball will then rebound off the cushion and jump over the reds to pot the black.

Stunts and Bottle Shots

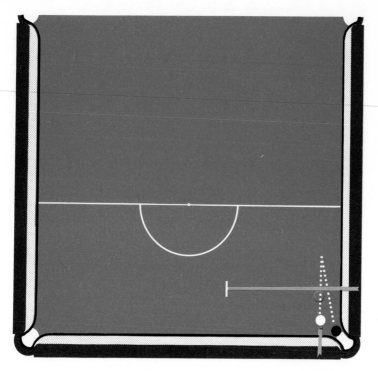

25 Rest shot In this trick you are trying to pot the black in the hardest possible way, making the cue ball jump over the red and the Rest to come back on to the black.

Strike the cue ball low down, from an elevated position, at the red. The cue ball will leap over the Rest and come back underneath it to pot the black ball.

26 Triangle shot   All tables play differently, so you will need a practice shot or two to see at what angle the yellow comes off the cushion.

The yellow and the inside red are against the cushion and the two other reds touching them. The cue ball is placed about 2ft away at an angle of 45° to the cushion.

Strike the cue ball low down at the red on the cushion. The yellow will then go diagonally across the table to the opposite corner pocket. The Triangle and four more reds are placed across this pocket, but the yellow will jump when it hits the base of the Triangle and go over the reds into the pocket.

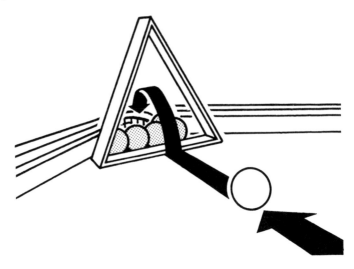

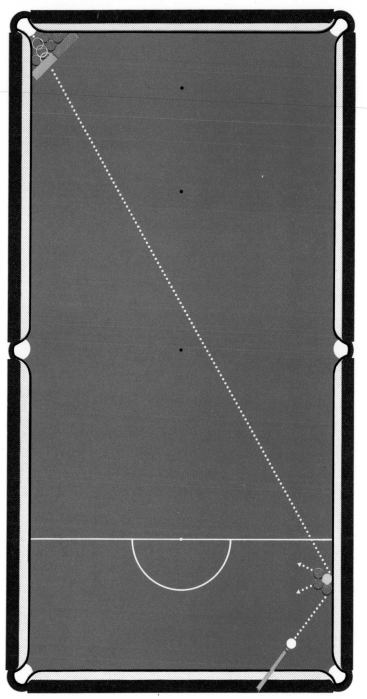

27 Jump shot (It is advisable to use an extra piece of cloth under the cue ball when attempting jump shots.)
You are potting the black by making the cue ball jump over the reds and through the Triangle.
Strike the cue ball above centre, hurtling it over the reds, through the Triangle with one bound and then on to the black.

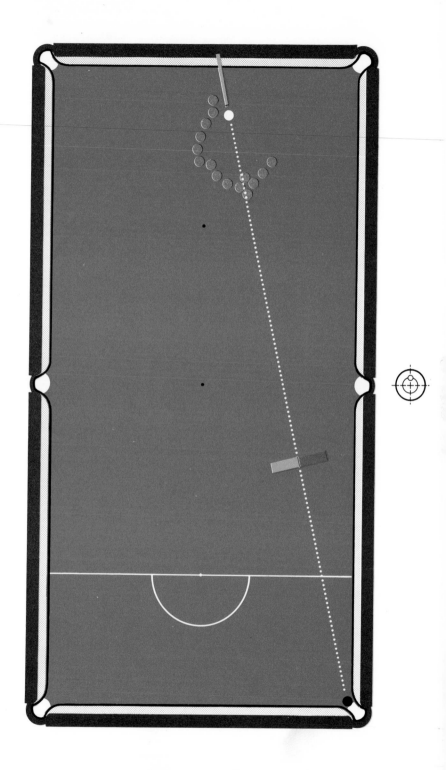

28 Paper bag shot   Lie a paper bag in the centre of the table with the opening facing the cue ball. Play gently towards the opposite centre pocket.

The paper bag will roll over with the weight of the ball so that the opening will be facing the opposite pocket when the ball emerges.

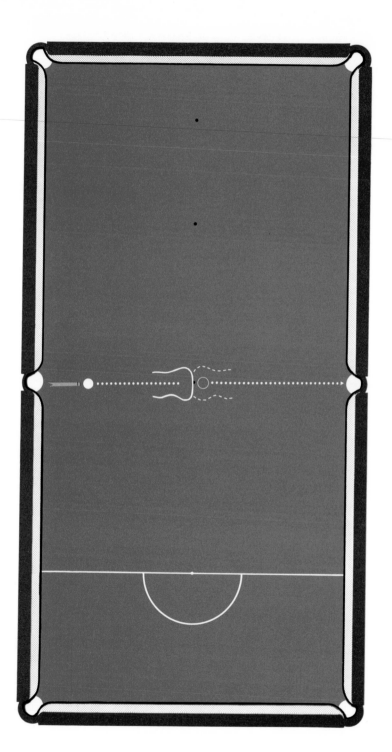

29 Steeplechase   Place four cues on the table with the butt ends so they all point towards the corner pocket — see the illustration — but note that the butt ends of the two inner cues overlap the lip of the pocket.

Strike the reds one by one, using right-hand side and a fair amount of power, so that they each rush round the table, climb up over the cues and drop into the pocket.

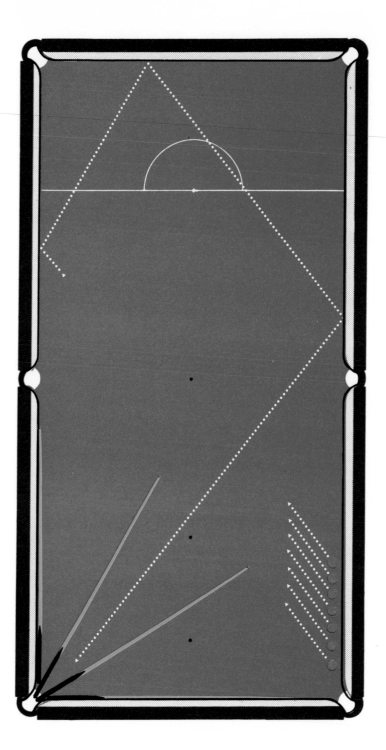

30 Tram-line shot   Place two cues together so that the butt ends are up against the back of the corner pocket, then align them with the centre pocket. Two further cues are placed along the cushions to keep the others in place.

Nos 1 and 2 reds are set against the angles of the centre pocket, with the blue touching No 1 red. A third red is placed over the top left-hand pocket.

Strike the cue ball on to the blue with sufficient power to take it right round the table. The blue will pot the red in the top pocket after potting No 1 red. The cue ball will go round the table, up on to the two cues and then trickle gently down them to pot No 2 red.

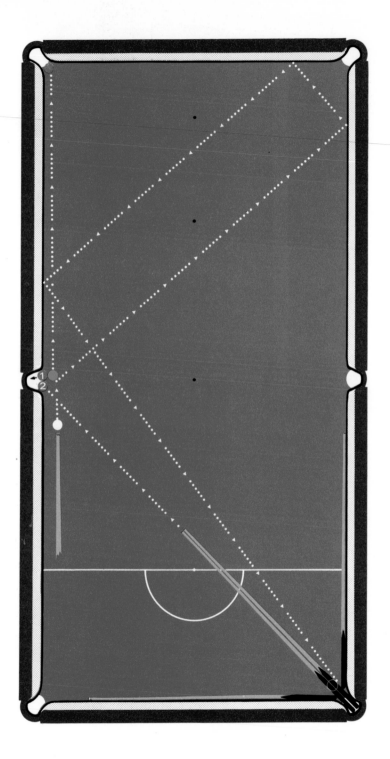

31 Flying cannon Place a ball on top of a bottle (disposable bottles break less easily), so that it sits on top of the opening; the red and the cue ball are then positioned roughly at right-angles.

The object is to make a cannon by going off the red on to the ball on top of the bottle — a shot that requires some nerve. Again, remember to use an extra piece of cloth when trying jump shots.

Come down on the cue ball, striking it above centre — and then get out the dustpan and brush.

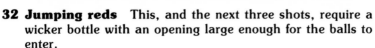

32 Jumping reds   This, and the next three shots, require a wicker bottle with an opening large enough for the balls to enter.

Get someone to hold the bottle firmly down and against the cushion. Take the nearest first, striking ball above centre and diagonally downward which will lift the ball off the table and into the bottle; then so on until all balls are potted in the bottle.

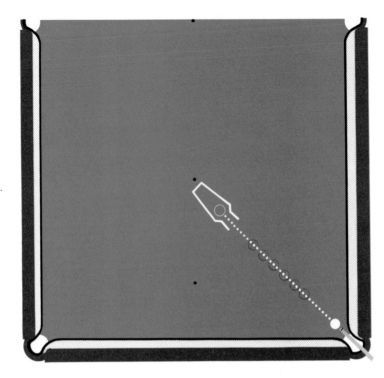

33 Hurdle bottle shot The principle here is very similar to the last shot, except that this time you are getting the cue ball to hurdle over a line of reds.

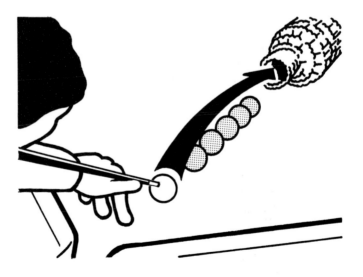

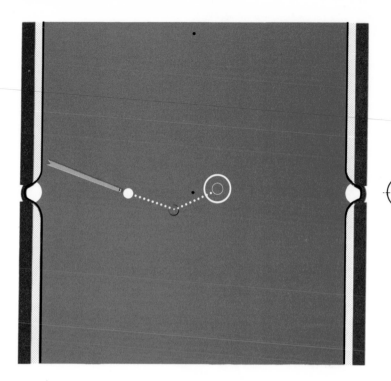

34 Bottle shot Again, this shot requires a wicker bottle. Come down on the ball, striking it above centre. The object is to pot the ball into the neck of the bottle.

35 Magic bottle shot   This is the shot I am always asked to do on T.V. shows. If you can do the other bottle shots you should be able to do this one, mind you none of them are easy.

First place a white ball so that it rests just inside the shoulder of the bottle. Then play a jump shot with the red, straight into the neck of the bottle. The force of the red going in will make the bottle spin round, thus ejecting the white.

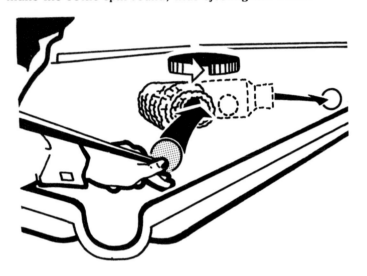

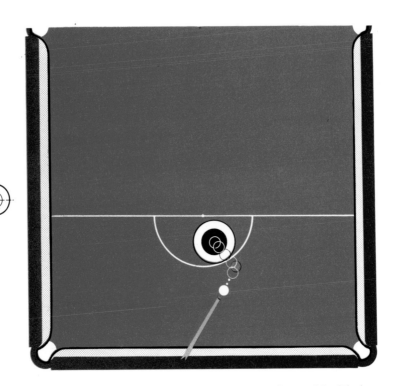

36 Bowler hat shot This shot is very similar to No 34, but much easier since the target is considerably bigger.

The bowler hat is placed on the table with the red and the cue ball approximately at right-angles. The object is to play off the red into the bowler hat.

Billiards Trick Shots

37 They all go down   Put the red on the pink spot and place a white touching it so that they are both aligned with the top right-hand pocket.

Position the cue ball as indicated in the illustration and play to go off red into the bottom pocket hitting the cue ball above centre. The red will then go into the centre pocket and the white into the top right-hand pocket.

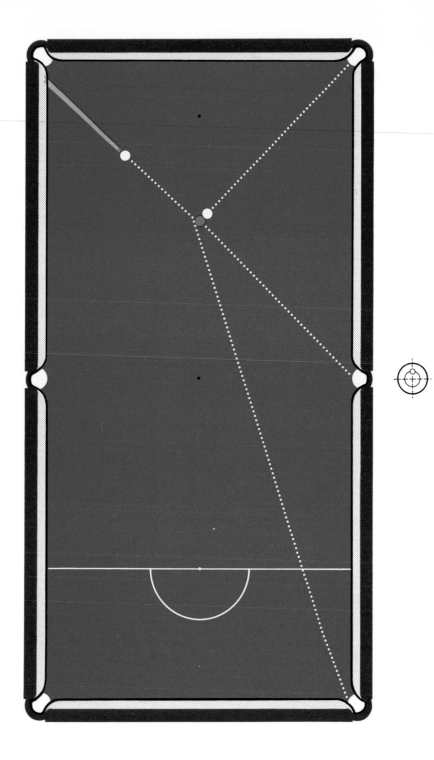

38 Disappearing shot Once again place the red on the pink spot, striking the cue ball just above centre, aim to go in-off white into the left-hand corner pocket. The red will follow into the same pocket while the white is potted in the right-hand corner.

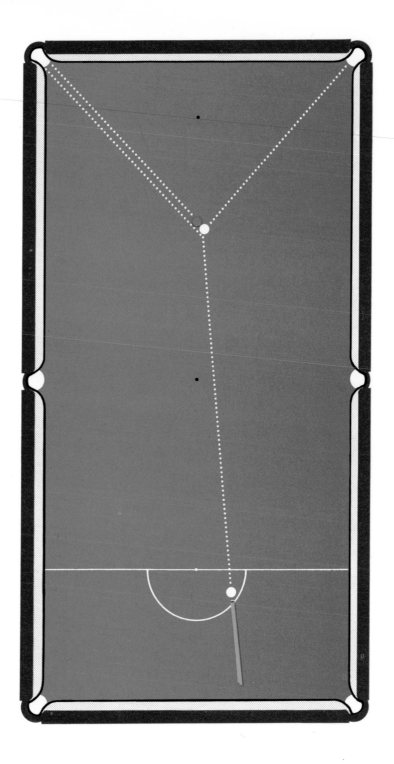

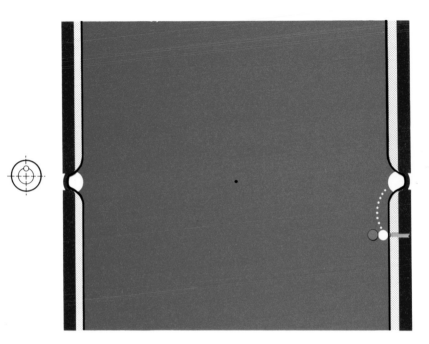

39 Massé shot The massé shot is played almost vertically downwards. In the situation shown in the illustration it is possible to go in-off red into the centre pocket using this technique.
Strike the cue ball downward, just short of centre, very sharply.

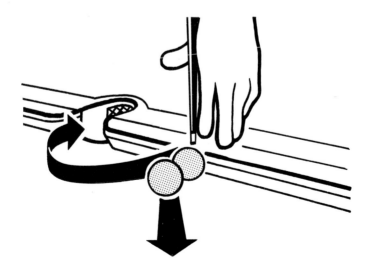

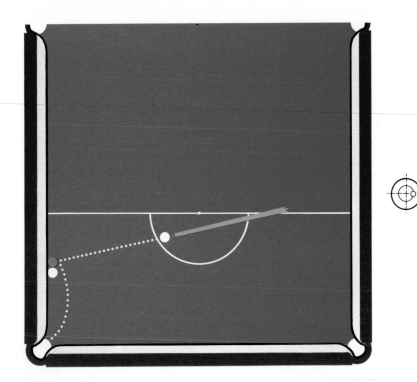

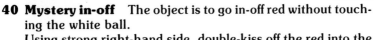

40 Mystery in-off The object is to go in-off red without touching the white ball.

Using strong right-hand side, double-kiss off the red into the corner pocket.

41 In-off red   (This shot can only be played against the nap on the cloth.)
Try to go in-off red into the bottom right-hand pocket. The shot requires strong follow-through using left-hand side.

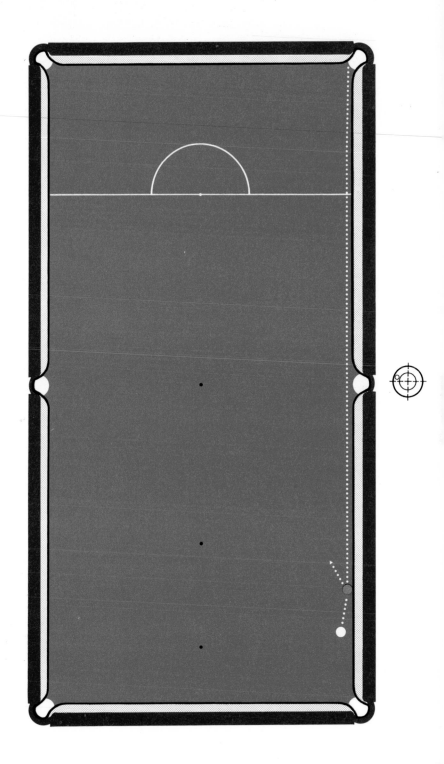

42 Double-kiss cannon Strike the cue ball low down, using screw with strong right-hand side to double-kiss off the red. The cue ball will then go round the table to make the cannon.

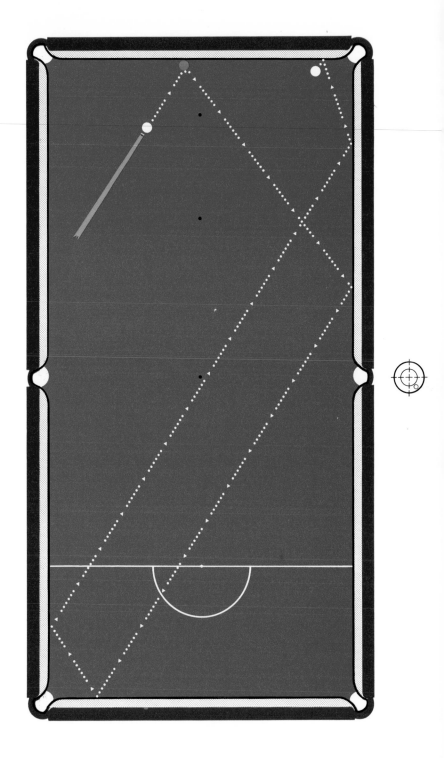

43 Two-cushion cannon   The red and white are placed near to the baulk line and touching each other. The cue ball is placed against the cushion and only a few inches from the red.

Using strong left-hand side on the cue ball, hit the red thinly to take the cue ball on to the side cushion, off the top cushion to meet the white near to the centre pocket.

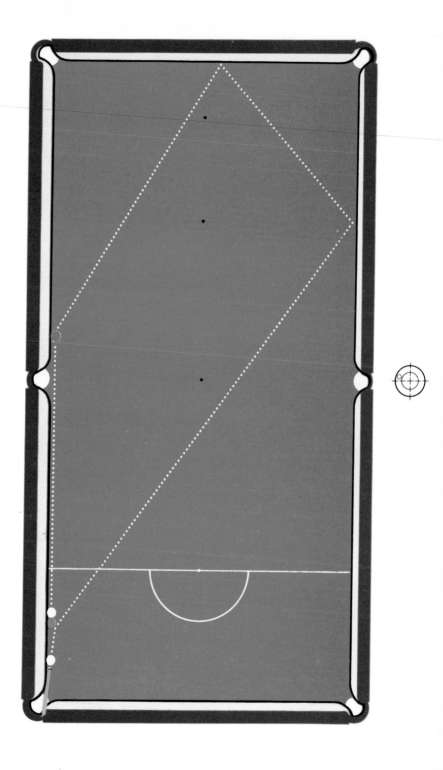

44 Three-cushion cannon   The red and white are placed in a similar position to the last shot. The cue ball, though, is positioned directly across the table from the red.

To make a three-cushion cannon, use strong left-hand side striking the red ball — at about quarter ball — fairly hard. The cue ball will then come off the baulk cushion and the side cushion to cannon on to the white ball near the top pocket.

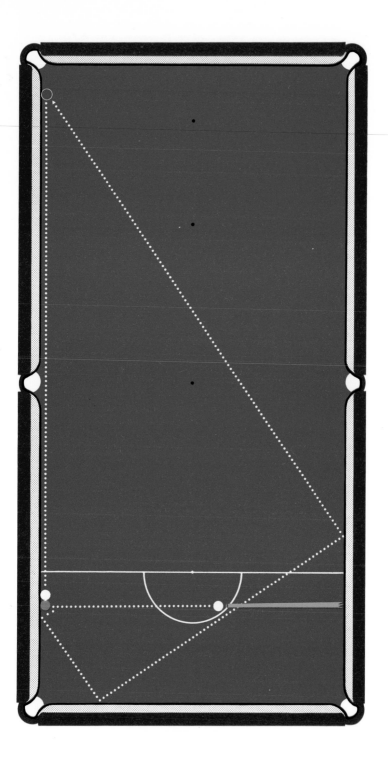

45 Five-cushion cannon   This is a beautiful cannon because the cue ball has to travel all the way around the table to make the shot.

Place the billiard balls as shown in the illustration, then strike the cue ball using right-hand side and making thin contact with the red. The cue ball will go off five cushions — or six if you are lucky — to make a superb cannon.

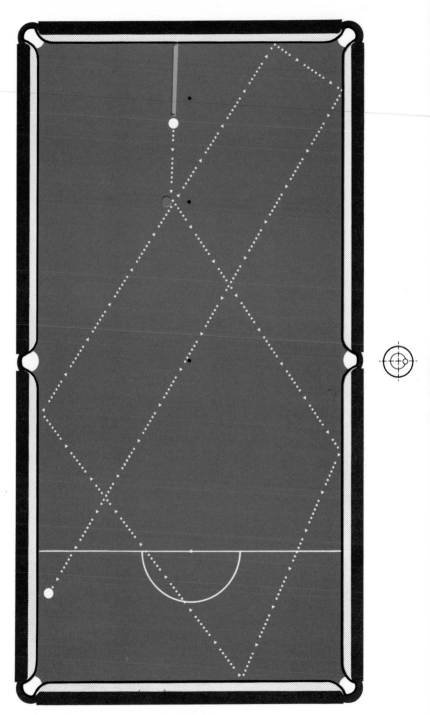

46 Five- (or six-) cushion cannon Strike the cue ball with plenty of power, using strong left-hand side to make the cannon off five cushions, or, again, six if you are lucky.

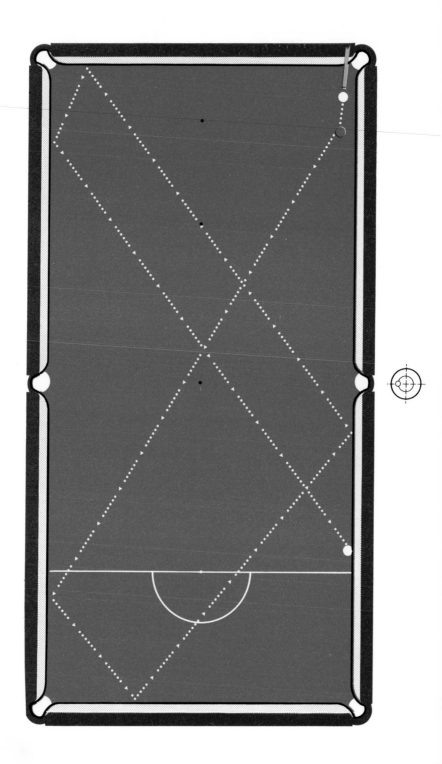

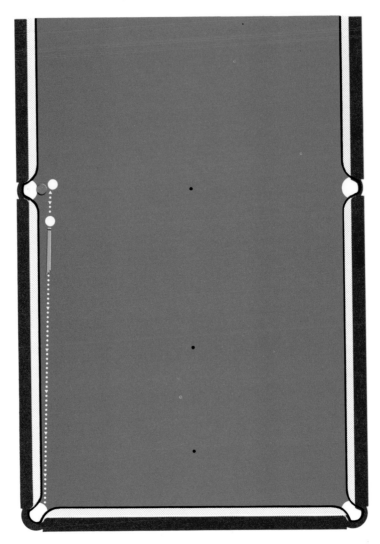

47 Seven shot This shot scores seven at billiards.
A deep screw shot off the white is required to take the cue
ball back to the top corner pocket, making a cannon and potting the red on the way.

48 Eight shot (1)   The object is to pot the red, screw back on to the white to make a cannon *and* go in-off — which would score eight.

Strike the cue ball below centre directly at the red. The cue ball will double-kiss off the red up the side cushion and go in-off into the centre pocket.

49 Eight shot (2) Again, a deep screw shot is required and also heavy right-hand side.

Pot the red, screw back on to the white and then, providing you have put enough screw on the cue ball, back up the table to the top corner pocket.

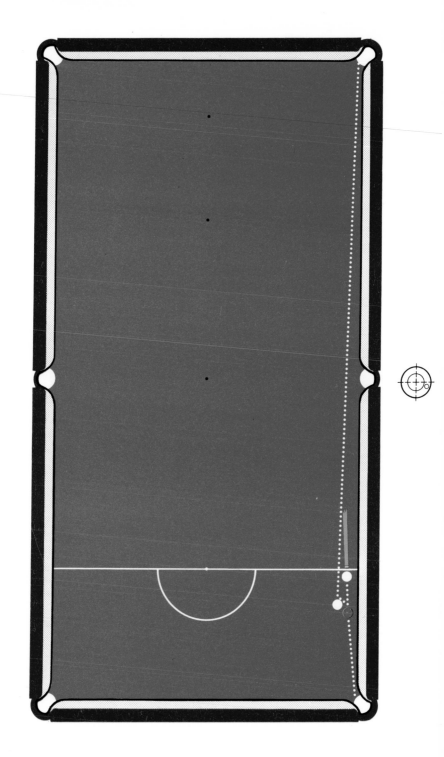

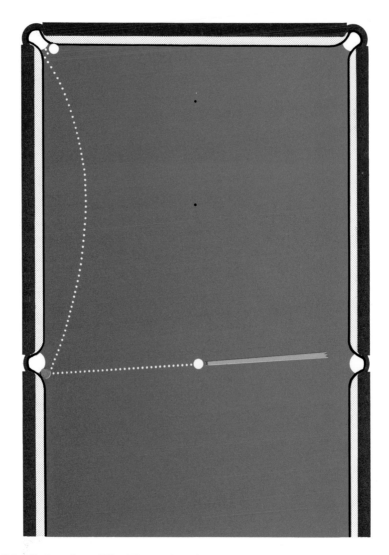

50 Eight shot (3) The red and the white are placed against the angles of the pockets, as shown in the illustration.
Using left-hand side, double-kiss off the red to pot it and take the cue ball up the table to make a cannon and go in-off white into the corner pocket.

An
Extra Touch

51 In-off, or pot, a moving ball Push the red ball up the table and try to go in-off it before it reaches the top cushion (left in the illustration). Then, try potting the red instead (right).

I hold both balls in my hand, letting go of the red and placing the white in one action.

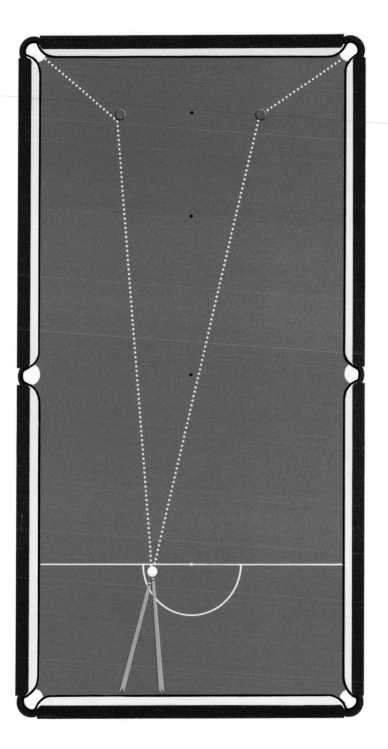

52 Miniature machine-gun shot This is the billiards version of the machine-gun shot and you will need to practise this if you are going to try the snooker version (No 54).

Place the two white balls and the red as illustrated (white on the green spot, the other white on the brown spot and the red on the yellow spot).

Strike the first white towards the corner pocket, then the second white and then the red so that the first white enters the pocket last. This shot requires great touch.

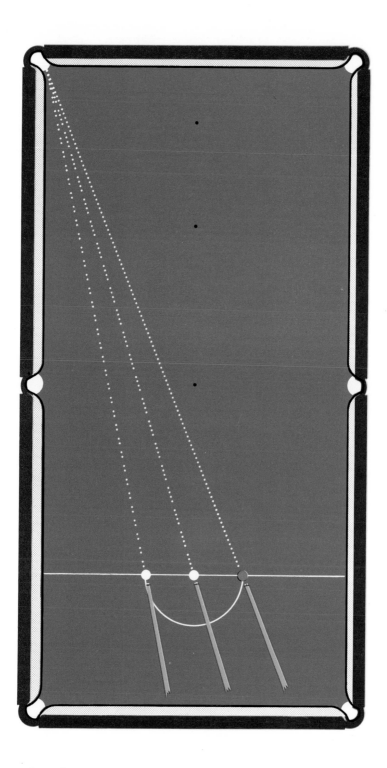

53 Final touch   Place the red ball over one of the top pockets and the cue ball near it, as shown in the illustration. Play as if to pot red off the baulk cushion, but before the cue ball reaches the red hit it again using deep screw. The cue ball will then go back a short distance down the table before the spin imparted by the second shot makes it double back to pot the red.

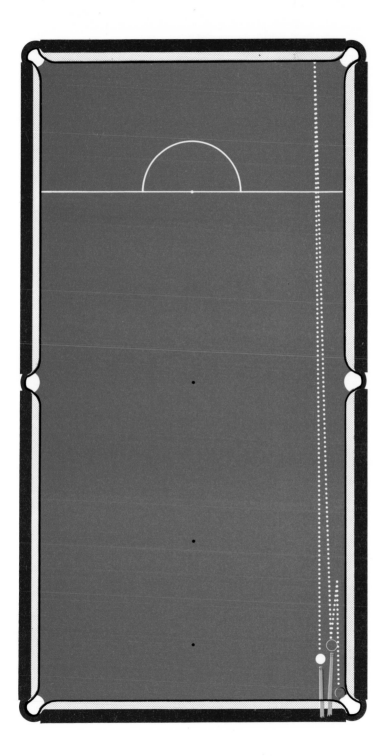

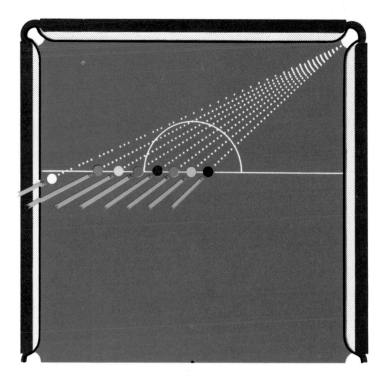

54 Machine-gun shot   This is a similar shot to No 51 but a great deal harder.

Line the seven colours up along the baulk line, spacing the balls about two inches apart from each other, but make sure to leave enough room for each to be potted in the corner pocket. You can place the cue ball wherever you like.

Before attempting the shot, test the speed of the table by striking the cue ball with just enough strength to pot it into the corner.

Now strike the cue ball first, and before it enters the pocket, pot all the colours into the same pocket.

The shot calls for a good cue action and excellent eyesight.